RICHARDS

LIST OF

PAMPHLETS, SONG BOOKS,

&c.

PAMPHLETS,

With beautiful coloured folding frontispieces, 6d. each.

Art of Legerdemain.
Bamfylde Moore Carew.
Baron Munchausen's Travels.
Buonaparte's Book of Fate.
Church-yard Gleanings.
Comical Budget of Fun and Frolic.
Cook, the Murderer.
Doctor Faustus.
Domestic Cookery, or the Housewife's Sure Guide.
Dream-book.
Dutchess of C——.
Gentleman's Valentine Writer.
George Barnwell.
Hoggart, the Murderer.
Jane Shore.
Lady's Valentine Writer.
Mary, the Maid of the Inn.
Nixon's Prophecies.
Norwood Gipsy.
True Lover's Own General Valentine Writer.
Turpin, the Highwayman.

————

SONG BOOKS.

PAMPHLET SONG BOOKS,

With beautiful coloured folding frontispieces, 6d. each.

Choice Songster.
Fashionable Songster.
New London Songster.
New Modern Minstrel.

New Universal Songster; or, Sportman's Companion.
Songster's Companion; or, Comical Budget.

WARBLERS,

With coloured folding frontispieces, 6d. each.

Comic and English Song-book.
Favourite New English Songs.
Little English Warbler.
New English Warbler.
New Collection of English Songs.
Popular English Songs.

SONG BOOKS,

With coloured frontispieces and titles, 6d. each.

The Nightingale.
The Skylark.
The Thrush.

————

Gentleman's New Fashionable Letter-Writer, 6d.
Lady's New Fashionable Letter-Writer, 6d.
Lady's and Gentleman's New Fashionable Letter-Writer, 1s.
Hoyle's Games; containing Whist, Chess, Draughts, and Back-Gammon, with the last new Rules established at London and Bath, 1s.

HODGSON'S EDITION.

THE KING

OF THE

BEGGARS,

OR THE HISTORY OF

Bampfylde Moore Carew

WHO WAS THE

SON OF A GENTLEMAN NEAR PLYMOUTH,

AND

Ran away from his Father and joined a

Gang of Gypsies,

DETAILING THE NUMEROUS

TRICKS AND IMPOSITIONS

Practised by him in various disguises,

WITH AN ACCOUNT OF

HIS CORONATION

AS

KING of the GYPSIES.

London:

ORLANDO HODGSON,

Carew joining the Beggars.   ...g Mad Tom.

Carew escaping fro...desertion.

THE KING OF THE BEGGARS.

Carew acting Mad Tom.

Carew flogged by Capt.ⁿ Tirade for desertion.

BAMFYLDE MOORE CAREW.

Carew joining the Beggars.

Carew escaping from Capt.ⁿ Harrison.

Pub.Aug.1.1823.by Hodgson &C.⁰ 10 Newgate Street.

THE
King of the Beggars;

OR, THE

Surprising Adventures

OF

BAMFYLDE MOORE CAREW:

WITH AN

ACCOUNT

OF HIS

TRAVELS & VOYAGES.

London:

PRINTED BY AND FOR HODGSON & CO.

No. 10, NEWGATE-STREET.

Sixpence.

THE
KING OF THE BEGGARS,

&c. &c.

THE county of Devon has to boast the birth of the famous Bamfylde Moore Carew, who was descended from a very reputable family, being the son of the Rev. Theodore Carew, of Bickley. He was born in July, 1693. Never was there known a more splendid appearance at any baptism: the Hon. Hugh Bamfylde, Esq. and the Hon. Major Moore, were his godfathers, both of whose names he bore; Mr. Bamfylde presented him with a piece of plate, whereon was engraved, in large letters, " BAMFYLDE MOORE CAREW."

At twelve years of age Bamfylde was sent to Tiverton school, where he acquired a very considerable knowledge in the Latin and Greek tongues; but soon a new exercise engaged his attention—this was hunting, in which he soon made a surprising progress; for he added to it a remarkable cheering halloo to the dogs ; and, besides this, found out a secret, hitherto unknown, of enticing any dog to follow him.

The Tiverton scholars had at this time the command of a fine pack of hounds, whereby he had frequent opportunities of gratifying his inclinations in that diversion.

It happened that a farmer, living in the country adjacent to Tiverton, who used to hunt with the Tiverton scholars, acquainted them of a fine deer which he had seen, with a collar about its neck, in the fields about his farm, which he supposed to be the favourite deer of some gentleman not far off: this was very agreeable news to the Tiverton scholars, who went in a great body to hunt it. This happened a short time before harvest; the chase was very hot, and they ran the deer many miles, which did great damage, the corn being almost ripe. Upon the death of the deer, and examination of the collar, it was found to belong to Colonel Nutcombe, of the parish of Clayhanger. The farmers and gentlemen complained very heavily to Mr. Rainer, the schoolmaster, of the havock made in their fields, when our hero, and three of his companions, being severely threatened, they absented themselves from school, and the next evening fell into company with a society of gipsies, who were feasting and carousing at the Brick-house, near Tiverton.

This society consisted of eighteen persons of both sexes, who met with a full purpose of merriment and jollity; and after a plentiful meal upon fowls, ducks, and other dainty dishes, the flowing cups of October, cyder, &c. went cheerfully round, and merry songs and country-dances crowned the jovial banquet; in short, so great an air of mirth and pleasure appeared in the faces of this society, that our youngsters from that time conceived a sudden inclination to enlist into their company; which, when they communicated it to the gipsies, they regarded it as only spoken in jest; but as they tarried all night in their company, and continued in the same resolution the next morning, they were at length induced to admit them into their number, the proper oaths being first administered.

Thus was Mr. Carew initiated into the mysteries of a society, which for antiquity needs give place to none. He did not continue long in it without being consulted in important matters; particularly by Madam Musgrove, of Monkton, near Taunton, who hearing of his fame, sent for him to consult in an affair of difficulty. When he was come, she informed him that she suspected a large quantity of money was buried somewhere about her house, and if he would acquaint her with the particular place, should reward him handsomely.

Our hero informed the lady, that under a laurel-tree in the garden lay the treasure she sought for, but that her planet of good fortune did not reign till such a day and hour, till which time she should desist from searching for it. The good lady rewarded him very generously with twenty guineas for his discovery.

In the mean time, his parents were not able to get the least tidings of him, though they publicly advertised him, and sent messengers to every part: till, at the expiration of a year and a half, his heart melted with tenderness, and he repaired to his father's house at Bickley, in Devonshire. Disguised both in habit and countenance, he was not at first known; but when he discovered himself, joy gushed out in full streams, stopping the power of speech: they bedewed his cheeks with tears, and imprinted them with their kisses.

For some time unsatisfied longings after the community of gipsies preyed on his mind; long did filial piety and his inclinations struggle for the victory; at length the last prevailed. One day, therefore, without taking leave of any of his friends, he directed his steps towards Brick-house, at Tiverton, when finding some of the gipsies there, he joined their company, to the great satisfaction of them all.

Being again admitted at the first general assembly of the gipsies, he was soon after sent out on a cruize upon their enemies. The first effort that occurred to his thoughts was, the equipping himself with an old pair of trowsers, enough of a jacket to cover his nakedness; stockings such as nature gave; shoes, which had leaks enough to sink a first-rate man-of-war; and a woollen cap, so black, that one might safely swear it had never been washed. He became now nothing more nor less than an unfortunate ship-wrecked seaman. In his first excursion, he gained a very considerable booty, having imitated the passes and certificates that were necessary for him to travel unmolested, and proceeded to Totness, and from thence to the city of Exeter, where he raised a contribution in one day, amounting to several pounds.

He next became the plain, honest, country farmer, who, living in the Isle of Sheppy, in Kent, had the misfortune to have his grounds overflowed, and all his cattle drowned. His habit was neat, but rustic; his air and behaviour simple and inoffensive; his speech in the Kentish dialect; his countenance dejected; his tale pitiful; his wife and seven tender helpless infants being partakers of his misfortunes; in short, never did actor personate any character more just, seldom getting less than a guinea a day.

He once gave a handsome gratuity to an expert and famous rat-catcher, (who assumed the honour of being rat-catcher to the king,) to be initiated into that art, and the still more useful secret of curing madness in dogs or cattle.

Our hero soon attained so considerable a knowledge in his profession, that he practised with much success and applause, to the great advantage of the public.

Forming a new stratagem, he exchanged his habit, shirt and all, for only an old blanket; shoes and stockings he laid aside, because they did not suit his present purpose. Being thus accoutred or rather unaccoutred, he was now no more than

" Poor Mad Tom, whom the foul fiend has led through fire and through flame, through ford and whirlpool, and quagmire, that hath laid knives under his pillow, and halters in his pew, set ratsbane by his porridge, made him proud at heart to ride on a bay-trotting horse over four-inch bridges, to curse his own shadow for a traitor; who eats the swimming frog, the toad, the tadpole, the wall-newt, and the water-newt; that in the fury of his heart, when the foul fiend rages, swallows the old rat and ditch dog, drinks the green mantle of the standing pool:

And mice, and rats, and such small geer,
Have been Tom's food for many a year!

In this character, and with such like expressions, he entered the houses of both great and small, claiming kindred to them, and committing all manner of frantic actions; by which means he raised very considerable contributions.

Our hero, having carried on his vagaries throughout England and Wales, was resolved to see other countries and manners. He found a ship ready to sail for Newfoundland, lying at Dartmouth, where he then was, and agreed to embark on board her. She was called the Atlantic, commanded by Captain Holdsworth.—Nothing remarkable happened in their passage which relates to our hero; we shall therefore pass by it, and land him safe in Newfoundland.

During the fishing-season, he visited all the settlements, both English and French, accurately making himself fully acquainted with the names, circumstances, and characters, of all the inhabitants of any note, on the great bank of Newfoundland, which is 450 miles in length.

The fishing season being over, our hero returned again in the Atlantic to Dartmouth, from whence he had first sailed, bringing with him a surprising fierce and large dog, which he had enticed to follow him, and made as gentle as a lamb, by an art peculiar to himself. Our hero was received with great joy by his fellow gipsies, and they were loud in his praises, when they understood he had undertaken this voyage to enable him to deceive their enemies with the greater success. He, accordingly, in a few days, went in the character of a shipwrecked seaman, homeward bound from Newfoundland, sometimes belonging to Pool, sometimes to other ports, and under such or such commanders, according as the newspapers gave accounts of such very melancholy accidents.

He now being able to give a very exact account of Newfoundland, the settlements, harbours, fishery, and inhabitants thereof, he applied, with great confidence to masters of vessels, and gentlemen well acquainted with those parts; so that those, whom before his prudence would not permit him to apply to, now became his gratest benefactors; as the perfect account he gave of the country engaged them to give credit to all he asserted, and made them very liberal.

It was in Newcastle-upon-Tyne that he became enamoured with the daughter of Mr. G—y, an eminent apothecary and surgeon there. This young lady had charms sufficient to captivate the heart of any man susceptible of love, and they made a very deep impression upon him. Our hero tried all love's persuasions with his fair one in an honourable way; and as his person was very engaging, and his appearance genteel, he did not find her greatly averse to his proposals. He passed with her for the mate of a collier's vessel, in which he was supported by Captain L—n, in whose vessel they set sail, and they had an exceeding quick passage to Dartmouth, where they landed. In a few days they set out for Bath, where they lawfully solemnized their nuptials, with great gaiety and splendour.

Our lovers began at length to be weary of the same repeated rounds of pleasure at Bath, they therefore paid a visit to the city of Bristol. After some stay there, they made a tour through Somersetshire, and Dorsetshire, into Hampshire, where they paid a visit to an uncle of our hero's living at Porchester, near Gosport, who was a clergyman of distinguished merit and character; here they were received with great politeness and hospitality, and staid a considerable time.

His uncle made him very lucrative offers, but he rejected them all, and began to prepare for his departure from his uncle's, in order to make some excursions on the enemy; and to do this he equipt himself in a black loose gown, put on a band, a large white peruke, and broad-brimmed hat; his whole deportment was agreeable to his dress; his pace was solemn and slow; his countenance thoughtful and grave, his eyes turned on the ground, but now and then raised in seeming ejaculations to heaven; in every look and action he betrayed his want; his behaviour excited the curiosity of many gentlemen, clergymen, &c. to enquire into the circumstances of his misfortunes. He acquainted them with his having exercised for many years the sacred office of a clergyman at Aberystwith, in Wales, but that the government changing, he had preferred quitting his benefice (though he had a wife and several children), to taking an oath contrary to his principles and conscience. This relation he accompanied with frequent sighs, deep marks of admiration of the ways of Providence, and warm expressions of his firm trust and reliance in his goodness and faithfulness, with high encomiums on the satisfaction of a good conscience. When he discoursed with any clergyman, or other persons of literature, he would now and then introduce some Latin or Greek sentences that were applicable to what he was talking of, which gave his hearers an high opinion of his learning; all this, and his thorough knowledge of those persons whom it was proper to apply to, made this stratagem succeed even beyond his own expectations.

Coming one day to 'Squire Portman's, at Brinson, near Blandford, in the character of a rat-catcher, and meeting in the court with Mr. Portman, the Rev. Mr. Bryant, and several other gentlemen, whom he well knew, he accosted them as a rat-catcher, asking if their honours had any rats to kill? "Do you understand your business well?" replies Mr. Portman. "Yes, and please your honour, I have been employed in his Majesty's yards and ships." "Well, go in and get something to eat, and after dinner we will try your abilities." After which he was called into a parlour, among a large company of gentlemen and ladies. "Well, honest rat-catcher," says Mr. Portman, "can you lay any scheme to kill the rats without hurting my dogs?" "Yes," replied Bamfylde, " I shall lay it where even the cats cannot climb to reach it."—" And what countryman are you?" " A Devonshire man, please your honour." " What's your name?" Our hero now perceiving that he was known, replied very composedly, " B-a-m-f-y-l-d-e M-o-o-r-e C-a-r-e-w." This occasioned a good deal of mirth; and Mr. Pleydell, of St. Andrew's Milbourne, expressed a pleasure at seeing the famous Bamfylde Moore Carew, saying, he had never seen him before. " Yes, but you have," replies he, " and given me a suit of clothes." Mr. Pleydell testified some surprise at this, and desired to know when it was. Mr. Carew asked him, if he did not remember a poor wretch meeting him one day at his stable-door, and that Mr. Pleydell asked him if he was mad; he replied, no; but a poor unfortunate man, cast away upon the coast, and taken up, with eight others, by a Frenchman; the rest of the crew sixteen in number being drowned; and that Mr. Pleydell gave him a guinea and a suit of clothes. Mr. Pleydell said, he well remembered such a poor object. " Well," replied our hero, " that object was no other than the expert rat-catcher now before you;" at which all the company laughed very heartily." " Well," says Mr. Pleydell, " I will lay a guinea I shall know you again come in what shape you may;" the same said Mr. Seymour, of Hantford. Some of the company asserting to the contrary of this, they desired our hero to try his ingenuity upon them.

Having received a handsome contribution of the company, he took his leave; but Parson Bryant followed him out, and acquainted him that the same company, and many more, would be at Mr. Pleydell's on such a day, and advised him to make use of that opportunity to deceive them altogether, which our hero resolved to do.

When the day was come, the barber was called in to make his face as smooth as art could do, and

oman's gown, and other female accoutrements, of
he largest size, were provided for him. In order to
nder his disguise more impenetrable, he borrowed
little hump-backed child of a tinker, and two more
f some others of his community. Thus accoutred,
nd thus hung with helpless infants, he went to Mr.
leydell's He had not been long there, before the
entlemen all came in together, who accosted him
ith, "Where did you come from, old woman?"
From Kirton, please your honours, where the
other of these poor helpless babes was burnt to
eath, and all they had consumed." "D—n you,"
aid one of the gentlemen, "there has been more
oney collected for Kirton than ever Kirton was
orth:" however, he gave this old grandmother a
hilling; the other gentlemen likewise relieved her.
ut the gentlemen were not got into the house, before
heir ears were saluted with a tantivee, tantivee, and
halloo to the dogs: upon which they turned about,
upposing it to be some brother sportsman, but see-
g nobody, Worthy Sir swore the old woman they
ad relieved was Carew; a servant was despatched
o bring her back into the parlour where she con-
essed who she was: the gentlemen were now em-
loyed in unskewering the children from his back,
nd observing the features and dress of this grand-
other, which afforded them sufficient entertainment;
hey afterwards rewarded him for the mirth he had
rocured them.

Our hero soon after this executed a very bold
ratagem upon his Grace the Duke of Bolton; being
itroduced into the hall, where the duke was to pass
rough, he had not being long there before the duke
me in; upon which he presented a petition, setting
rth, That the unfortunate petitioner, Bamfylde
oore Carew, was supercargo of a vessel that was
 st away coming from Sweden, in which he lost his
hole effects. The duke seeing the name of Bamfylde
oore Carew, treated him with respect, and called

a servant to conduct him into a room, where the duke's barber waited on him to shave him; and after came in a footman, who brought in a good suit of trimmed clothes, a fine Holland shirt, and all other parts of dress suitable to these. On his departure the duke made him a present of fifty pounds.

He set out next morning for Salisbury; here he presented his petition to the mayor, bishop, and other gentlemen of great note and fortune, and acquainted them with the favours he had received from his Grace the Duke of Bolton. The gentlemen having occular demonstration of the duke's liberality, relieved him very generously. With the same success, he visited Lord Arundell, Sir Edward Bouverie, and many other gentlemen in the counties of Wilts, Dorset and Somerset. Being one morning near the seat of his great friend, Sir William Courtenay, he was resolved to pay him three visits that day; he goes, therefore to a house frequented by his order, and there pulls off his fine clothes, and put on a parcel of rags; in this dress he got half-a-crown of that gentleman, as a man that had met with misfortunes at sea; at noon he puts on a leather apron, a coat which seemed scortched by the fire, and was then relieved as an unfortunate shoemaker, who had been burnt out of his house, and lost all he had; in the afternoon he goes again in his trimmed clothes, and repeats his misfortune as a supercargo of a vessel which had been cast away, and his whole effects lost, at the same time mentioning the kindness he had received from his Grace the Duke of Bolton. Sir William generously relieved him, presenting him with a guinea at his departure.

It was about this time the old king of the gipsies, named Clause Patch, well known in most parts of England, finished a life spent in promoting the welfare of his people. A little before his death, finding his final dissolution approach, he called together all his children, to the number of eighteen, and sum

oned as many of his subjects as were within any
nvenient distance, being willing that the last spark
his life should go out in the service of his people.
n the day appointed, a great number assembled
gether.

The venerable old king was brought in a high
air, and placed in the midst of them, his children
anding next to him, and his subjects behind them.
or some time the king of the mendicants sat con-
mplating the tender emotions of his subjects, then
nding forward, he thus addressed them :—

"Children and friends, I regard you all with a paternal love, I have
en you from your daily employments, that you may eat and drink with
before I die; but before you depart, the books shall be examined, and
ery one of you shall receive from my private purse the same sum that
made by your business this day of the last week; let not this act of
erosity displease my heirs—it is the last waste I shall make of their
res; the rest I die possessed of is their's of right; but my council,
ugh directed to them only, shall be for the general good of all. The
od success, my dear children, with which my industry has been blessed,
given me the power of bestowing one hundred pounds on each of you—
mall fortune, but improveable; and of most use, as it is a proof that
ery one of you may gain as much as the whole, if your idleness or vice
rent not; mark by what means! Our community, like people of all
ofessions, live upon the necessities, the passions, or the weakness of our
low-creatures. The two great passions of the human breast are vanity
d piety; both these have great power in men's actions; but the first is
ater far, and he who can attract these the most successful will gain the
gest fortune. A real scene of affliction moves few hearts to pity; dis-
bled wretchedness is what finds its way to the human mind, and I am
t dissembling. Take, therefore, among you, the maxims I have laid
wn for my own guide, and use them with as much success as I have done.
"Trouble not yourselves about the nobility—affluence has made them
in and insensible; they cannot pity what they can never feel.
"Some people show you in their looks the whole thoughts of their hearts,
d give you a fine notice how to act with them; if you meet a sorrowful
untenance with a red coat, be sure the wearer is a disbanded officer;
a female attack him, and tell him she is the widow of a poor marine,
o had served twelve years and then broke his heart because he was
ned out without a penny; if you see a plain man hang down his head
he comes out of a nobleman's gate, tell him—Good worthy sir, I beg
r pardon, but I am a poor ruined tradesman, that was once in good
iness, but the people would not pay me. And if you see a pretty woman
h a dejected look, send your first sister that is at hand to complain of
ad husband, that gets drunk and beats her, and has spent all her sub-
nce. There are but two things that can make a handsome woman
ancholy—the having a bad husband, or the having no husband at all;
the first of these is the case, one of the former crimes will touch her to

" Trouble not yourselves about the nobility—affluence has made them in and insensible ; they cannot pity what they can never feel.

" Some people show you in their looks the whole thoughts of their hearts, give you a fine notice how to act with them ; if you meet a sorrowful untenance with a red coat, be sure the wearer is a disbanded officer ; a female attack him, and tell him she is the widow of a poor marine, o had served twelve years and then broke his heart because he was ned out without a penny ; if you see a plain man hang down his head he comes out of a nobleman's gate, tell him—Good worthy sir, I beg r pardon, but I am a poor ruined tradesman, that was once in good iness, but the people would not pay me. And if you see a pretty woman h a dejected look, send your first sister that is at hand to complain of d husband, that gets drunk and beats her, and has spent all her substance. There are but two things that can make a handsome woman ancholy—the having a bad husband, or the having no husband at all ; the first of these is the case, one of the former crimes will touch her to

the quick, and loosen the stringes of her purse; if the other, let a see
distressed object tell her, that she was to have been married well, but t
her lover died a week before; one way or other the tender heart of a fem
will be melted, and the reward will be handsome. If you meet a hom
but dressed up lady, pray for her lovely face, and beg a penny; if you
a mark of delicacy, by the drawing up of the nose, send somebody to sh
her a sore-head, a scald-head, or a rupture. If you happen to fall in w
a tender husband leading his big wife to church, send some companion t
has but one arm or two thumbs, or tell her of some monstrous child y
have brought forth, and the good man will pay you to be gone; if
gives but slightly, it is but following, getting before the lady, and talki
louder, and you may depend upon searching his pockets to better purpo
a second time. Many more things there are I have to speak of, but
feeble tongue will not allow me to speak them; profit by these, they w
be found sufficient, and if they prove to you, my children, what they h
been these eighteen years to me, I shall not repine at my dissoluti
As I find the lamp of life is not quite extinguished, I shall employ
little that remains in saying a few words of my public conduct as yo
king; I call you to witness, that I have loved you all with a pater
love; these now feeble spirits and limbs have been worn out in providi
for your welfare; and often have these now dim eyes watched, wh
your's have slept, with a father's care for your safety. I call you all
witness, that I have kept an impartial register of your actions, and
merit has passed unnoticed; I have with a most exact hand, divided
every one his share of our common stock, and have had no worth
favourite, or useless officer, to eat the honey of your labor. And for
these I have had my reward, in seeing the happiness, and having the l
of all my subjects. I depart, therefore, in perfect peace, to rest with
fathers; it remains, that I give you my last advice, which is, that
choosing my successor, you pay no partial regard to my family, but el
him only who is most worthy to rule over you."

He said no more, but leaning back in his cha
expired without a sigh.

When the day of election came, our hero w
chosen by a considerable majority, and was hail
by the whole assembly King of the Mendicants: t
public register of their actions being brought to hi
and committed to his care, and homage done him
the assembly. The whole concluded with gre
feasting and rejoicing.

Our hero, notwithstanding the particular privileg
of his office, was as active in his stratagems as eve
Being in the parish of Fleet, near Portland-race,
Dorsetshire, he heard of a ship in imminent dang
of being cast away. Early in the morning, befo
it was light, he pulls off his clothes, which he flu
into a pit, and then, unseen by any one, swims to t

ship, which now parted asunder; he found only one of the crew alive who was hanging by his hands at one side of the vessel. Mr. Carew immediately offered him his assistance to get him to shore, at the same time inquiring the name of the vessel and her master, what cargo was on board, whence she came, and whither bound? The poor wretch had no sooner answered his questions, than a sea broke upon the wreck, and overwhelmed him in the great deep. Mr. Carew being an excellent swimmer, he, with great difficulty got on shore, though not without hurt, the sea throwing him with great violence on the beach, whereby one of his arms was wounded. By this time a great number of spectators were gathered on the strand, who rejoiced to see Mr. Carew come on shore alive, supposing him to be one of the poor wretches belonging to the ship.

Among the spectators was the house-keeper of Madam Mohun, who gave him a handkerchief to bind up his wound, bade him follow her to her mistress's house, were she seated him before a good fire, and gave him some brandy, a shirt, and other apparel. She went up stairs, and acquainted her lady, in the most moving manner, with the whole affair. Her mistress immediately ordered a bed to be warmed for him, and took the greatest care of him; and Mr. Carew lay very quiet for three or four hours; then waking, he seemed to be very much disturbed in his mind. The good people of the house seeing this, brought him a good suit of clothes, and he got up; being told that the bodies of some of his ship-mates were flung on shore, he seemed greatly affected. Having received from Justice Farewell a guinea, and a passport for Bristol, with considerable contributions to the amount of nine or ten pounds, he expressed a desire to make the best of his way to Bristol; and the good Justice Farewell lent him his own horse to ride as far as Dorchester, and the parson of the parish sent his man to show him the way.

Going one day to pay a visit to Mr. Incledon Barnstaple, Devon; knocking at the door softly, was opened by the clerk, who accosted him with th common salutations of—How do you do, Mr. Carew where have you been? He readily replied, that h had been making a visit to 'Squire Bassett's, and i his return had called to pay his respects to M Incledon; the clerk very civilly asked him to wal in; but no sooner was he entered, than the door wa shut upon him by Mr. Justice Lethbridge, who ha concealed himself behind it, and Mr. Carew wa made prisoner.

He had sometime before this, in the shape of poor lame cripple, frightened either the justice o his horse, on Pilton-bridge. The justice vowed re venge, and now exulted greatly at having got him i his power. Fame had no sooner sounded her hun dred tongues that our hero was in captivity, but th justice's house was crowded with intercessors fo him; however, Justice Lethbridge was deaf to all At length a warrant was made out for conveying him to Exeter, and lodging him in one of the secures places in the city. The next day he was conducte to Exeter, here he was securely lodged for more tha two months, and brought up to the quarter session held at the castle when Justice Bevis was chairman Being asked by the chairman what parts of th world he had been in; he answered, Denmark Sweden, Muscovy, France, Spain, Portugal, New foundland, Ireland, Wales, and some part of Scot land? the chairman then told him, that he must pro ceed to a hotter country. He inquired into wha climate, and being told Maryland, he, with grea composure, said that it would save him five pound for his passage, as he was desirous of seeing tha country.

Soon after he was conducted on board the Julian Captain Froade commander. After a good voyag they arrived at Hampton, and entered Miles'-rive and cast anchor in Talbot county. The captain ordered all the men-prisoners to be close shaved against the next morning, and public notice to be given of the day of sale, and the prisoners were all ordered upon deck, where a large bowl of punch was made, and the planters flocked on board to purchase.—The punch went merrily round, and in the midst of their mirth, Mr. Carew thought it no breach of good manners to take an opportunity of slipping away, without taking leave of them.

Mr. Carew congratulated himself on his happy escape and deliverance; but, as he was travelling through the country, he was taken by four timbermen, who carried him before a justice, that committed him to New Town goal. Captain Froade, hearing of his being there, came and demanded him as a runaway. He sent round his long boat, paid all costs, and brought him once more on board his ship. The captain in a tyrannic tone bade him strip, calling to the boatswain to bring up the cat o' nine tails, and tie him to the main gears; after undergoing this cruel punishment, he took him on shore to a blacksmith, and had a heavy iron collar placed round his neck, which in Maryland they call a pot-hook, and is generally put on the necks of runaway slaves.

One night when all were asleep, Carew let himself down into a boat that was along-side, and made his escape into the woods; he travelled till he came to the Friendly Indians, who treated him kindly, and sawed off his iron collar. He one night seized one of their canoes, and pushing from the shore landed near Newcastle, in Pennsylvania.

The first house he went to was a barber's, of whose assistance he had great need. He told a moving story, saying, his name was John Elworthy of Bristol, that he had been artfully kidnapped by one Samuel Bull of the same place, and gone through great hardships in making his escape. The barber, willingly lent him his assistance in taking off his beard, during the operation they had a deal of discourse, the barber telling him his father came from Exeter, and presented him with a half-crown bill, and recommended him to one Mr. Wiggil, a quaker, of the same place, to whom he told the same moving story, and obtained a ten shilling bill from that same gentleman, and a recommendation to the rest of the quakers in the place, from whom he received a great deal of money.

Mr. Wiggil recommended him to a Captain Read, who was ready to sail, but Carew having a curiosity to see more of the country, thought proper to leave Pennsylvania without taking leave of his good friends. From hence he entered Buckingham county, where he inquired for George Boon, who formerly lived at Bradnich, in Devon. Here he went by his own name, telling him he had been taken prisoner, and carried into the Havannah, where he had lain many months.

At New London, he inquired if there were none of the name of Davey in that city? saying, they were near heirs to a fine estate near Crediton, in Devon, formerly belonging to Sir John Davey. He was then shewn to two ancient sisters of Sir John Davey, whose sons were timber men. He told them Sir J. Davey was dead, and his eldest son also, who had left two sons; that the younger brother, Humphrey Davey, was then living at Creedy-house. They then gave him two letters to deliver to Mr. Humphrey Davey; after which, each gave him a guinea, with recommendations to Captain Rogers, who was bound for England, with whom he embarked.

Being safely arrived, he travelled to Bristol, and then made the best of his way to the Mendicant's-hall, on Milehill. Just as he came there, the landlady clapped her hands, and swore it was either Carew or his ghost. Our hero's first inquiry was, when they had seen his dear wife; the landlady told him, that she had not seen her lately, but had heard that both she and his daughter were well.

He afterwards visited Exeter, and meeting Sir Harry Northcote, Dr. Andrews, and two other gentlemen, he accosted them with " God bless you, gentlemen." Sir Harry, staring very wistfully at him, cried, " Are you flesh and blood?—why, you never have been in America!" Dr. Andrews then asked if it was Carew. The report being spread that he was in Exeter, drew a number of spectators to see him, and, among the rest, Merchant Davey, who asked him in a great hurry, if the ship was cast away? "No, no," says he; " I have been in America; have had the honour to see your factor, Mr. Mean, and saw Griffiths sold for a thousand weight of tobacco; but did not I tell you I should be back before Captain Froade?" Mr. Davey asked him if he had been sold before he ran away? and on his replying that he had not, the merchant told him, jeeringly, that he was his servant still—that he should charge him five pounds for his passage, and five pounds for costs and charges, besides Captain Froade's bill. He next enquired, where he had left Captain Froade; Carew told him, in Miles'-river. The gentlemen then gave him money, as did likewise Mr. Davey.

Two months after this Captain Froade arrived, laden with tobacco. As soon as he came to an anchor, several gentlemen of Exeter going on board, inquired where he left Mr. Carew? " D——n him," replied the captain, " you'll never see him again— he ran away, was taken, put into New-Town goal, brought back, and whipped; had a pot-hook put on him, ran away with it about his neck, and was never heard of since." They told the captain he had been at home two months, which he swore could never be; however, they soon convinced him that it was so.

Soon after this, Mr. Carew went and paid his respects to Sir William Courtenay, returning him thanks

for what he had supplied him with when he sailed
for Maryland. Sir William and his brother, Mr
Henry Courtenay, conducted him into a noble parlour
where there was a large company of ladies, whom
our hero accosted with great respect. Sir William
then put a piece of money into his hat, as did Mr.
Courtenay, and bid him go round to the ladies, which
he did, addressing them in a very handsome manner;
and we need not add, gathered in a very plentiful
harvest.

The next day, at Moll Upton's, in Newton Bushel,
he met a sister of the order of mendicants; and he,
having an inclination to pay a visit at Sir Thomas
Carew's, at Hackam, soon made an agreement to
change habits for that day. The barber was then
sent for to make his face as smooth as his razor could
make it, and his hair was dressed with ribbons.
Thus metamorphosed, our hero sets out, having a
wand in his hand, and a little dog under his arm.
Being come to Sir Thomas Carew's, he rushes into
the house without ceremony, demanding his rent in
an imperious tone. The servants first ran one way,
then another; but he taking no notice of the confusion, continued to act the mad woman, beating his
head against the wall, kissing his dog, and demanding his rent. At last comes one of the women-
servants, saying, " Lady, you are welcome to your
rent," and gave him half-a-crown; but he was not to
be got rid of so easily: for now he fell a raving
again, and demanded some merry-go-down; upon
which they brought him some ale, which having
drank, took his leave, thanking them with a very low
curtsey.

He once put on the dress of a gentleman, and
went to a cock-match, at Plymouth, and betted
several wagers with Sir Coventry Carew, and his
own brother, of whom he had the good fortune to win.

About this time he put on a jacket and a pair of
trowsers, and made the best of his way to the seat

of Sir William W——m, near Watchet, and met Sir William, Lord Bolingbroke, and several other gentlemen and clergy, with some commanders of vessels, walking in the park. Carew approached Sir William with a great deal of seeming respect; and acquainted him he was a Silverton man; that he was the son of one of his tenants, named Moore; had been to Newfoundland, and in his passage homeward, the vessel was run down by a French ship in a fog, and only him and two more were saved; but, being put on board an Irish vessel, were carried into Ireland, and from thence landed at Watchett. Sir William asked him many questions concerning the inhabitants of Silverton, to all of which Carew gave satisfactory answers. Sir William at last asked him, if he knew Bickley, and if he knew the parson thereof? Carew replied, that he knew him very well, (and so indeed he might, as it was no other than his own father!) Sir William then inquired, what family he had? and whether he had not a son named Bamfylde? and what became of him? " Your honour," replied he, " means the beggar and dog-stealer: I don't know what is become of him, but it is a wonder if he is not hanged by this time." " No, I hope not," replied Sir William, " I should be glad, for his family's sake, to see him at my house." Sir William generously relieved him with a guinea, and Lord Bolingbroke followed his example; the other gentlemen and clergy contributed according to their different ranks.

Some time after this, he went to Boulogne, and then proceeded to Paris, and other noted cities of France, pretending to be a Roman Catholic, who had left England, his native country, out of an ardent zeal for spending his days in the bosom of the Catholic church. This story readily gained belief, and handsome contributions were made for him. With a little change of habit, he used to address the English residents, as a protestant and shipwrecked seaman; and had the good fortune to meet with an English

physician at Paris, to whom he told his deplorable
tale, who not only relieved him, but recommended
him to that noble pattern of benevolence, Mrs. Hor-
ner, from whom he received ten guineas, and from
some other company with five more. After that
Carew returned to England, and being in the city of
Exeter with his wife, walking upon the quay there,
he was apprehended by Merchant D—y, accompanied
by several captains of vessels. He found it in vain
to resist, as he was overpowered by numbers, and
therefore desired to be carried before some magistrate;
but this was not hearkened to, for they forced him on
board a boat, which carried him to the Philleroy,
Captain Simmonds, bound for America, with convicts.

The wind coming fair, they hoisted sail, and soon
bade adieu to the English coast. After they had
been at sea a few days, Captain Simmonds died, and
Harrison the mate took the command of the ship.
Our hero now had the liberty of coming upon deck,
where the captain entered into conversation with him,
and jocosely asked him, if he thought he should be
at home before him. He answered he thought he
should, at least he would endeavour to be so. After
sixteen weeks passage, they made the coast of
America, and entered Miles'-river. Here they fired
a gun, and the captain went on shore; in the mean
time the men-prisoners were ordered to be close
shaved, and the women's heads to be shaved, and the
women to have clean caps on. This was scarcely
done, before an overseer, belonging to Mr. Bennet,
in Way-river, and several planters, came off to buy
the prisoners. Some of the planters knew Carew
again, and cried out, " Is not this the man Captain
Froade brought over, and put a pot-hook upon?"
" Yes," replied Harrison, with a great oath " and
I'll take care he shall not be at home before me."

During this, Carew observing a great many canoes
and boats lying alongside the vessel, took an opportunity, when it grew dark, of slipping down the ship's

side into one of them, with which he paddled towards the shore. He had not gone far, before the noise he made gave an alarm. Harrison immediately called out, " Where is Carew?" and being told he was gone off, swore he would rather have lost half of the prisoners than him. All hands were now called upon to pursue; the captain and planters left the bowl; the river was covered with canoes, and every thing was in confusion. Carew was within hearing of this, but had the good fortune to get on shore before any of them; he immediately took himself to the woods, and climbed up into a tree, where he had not been many minutes, before he heard the captain, sailors, and planters, all in pursuit of him.

As soon as they were gone, he began to reflect on his present situation, and at last resolved to steer farther up into the woods, which he accordingly did, and got up another tree, where he sat the succeeding day without food. The next day, towards night, he was almost spent for want of food; when happening to espy a planter's house at some distance, he was resolved to venture down in the night. Accordingly he went into the planter's yard, where he found some milch-cows, which he milked into his hat, making a most delicious feast. Having found out this method of subsisting, he proceeded forward in the same manner, till the morning of the eleventh day, when he came in sight of Duck's-creek. Being afraid he might fall into the hands of his pursuers, he staid all the day in a tree, and at night came to the water-side to see for a canoe, but found them all chained; he therefore caught a horse, and making a sort of bridle with his handkerchief, swam him over to the opposite side. He then set off again, and living by begging, came to an old friend of his, who was surprised at seeing him there. He then told him in what manner he had been served; the other pitied him, and paid his passage to England, where he arrived at Bristol, and made the best of his way to Exeter. Fame

having sounded the arrival of our hero, several gentlemen flocked to the Oxford Inn to visit him, and
among the rest Merchant Davey.

The next morning, accompanied by his wife and
daughter, he paid his respects to Sir Thomas Carew at
Hackam, who received him with great kindness. Sir
Thomas told him, if he would decline the mendicant
order, he would take care to provide for him and his
family.

On his return home, he reflected how idly he had
spent the prime of life. These cogitations so con-
tinually wrought in him, that he came to a resolution
of resigning the Egyptian sceptre. The assemby
finding him determined, reluctantly acquiesced, and
he departed amid the applauses and sighs of his
subjects.

CANT PHRASES USED BY BEGGARS.

Abram, naked, without clothes; or scarce enough to cover their nakedness.—*Ambidexter*, one that goes snacks in gaming with both parties; also
a lawyer that takes fees of a plaintiff and defendant at once.—*Back'd*,
dead.—*Balsam*, money.—*Bandog*, a bailiff, or his follower.—*Barnacles*, the
irons worn in gaols by felons.—*Calle*, a cloak, or gown.—*Comefa*, a shirt
or shift.—*Cank*, dumb.—*Cauniken*, the plague.—*Cap*, to swear.—*Dace*,
two-pence.—*Dag*, a gun.—*Damber*, a rascal.—*Dancers*, stairs.—*Darkness*,
night.—*Dash*, a tavern-drawer,—*Facer*, a bumper without lip room.—
Fumens, hands.—*Fastner*, a warrant.—*Flue*, the recorder of London, or
any other town.—*Gan*, a mouth.—*Gamus*, the lips.—*Gage* a pot or pipe.—
George, a half-crown piece.—*Gigger*, a door.—*Half-nab*, at a venture, un-
sight unseen, hit or miss.—*Halfhead*, a sixpence.—*Hams*, breeches.—
Jackadandy, a little impertinent insignificant fellow.—*Jack-adams*, a fool.—
Ken, a house.—*Kicks*, breeches.—*King's pictures*, money.—*Laced mutton*,
a woman.—*Lamb-skin Men*, the judges of several courts.—*Maunders*,
beggars.—*Megs*, guineas.—*Nobbing chents*, the gallows—*Nutcrackers*, the
pillory.—*Ogles*, eyes.—*One in ten*, a parson.—*Panum*, bread.—*Panter*, a
heart.—*Quail-pipe*, a woman's tongue.—*Ruffin*, the devil.—*Rumbo*, a prison
or goal.—*Seedy*, poor, moneyless, exhausted.—*Smear*, a painter or plasterer.
—*Top-driver*, a lover of women.—*Topping-cheat*, the gallows.—*Vampers*,
stockings.—*Velvet*, a tongue.—*Wattles*, ears.—*Whids*, words.—*Whouhall*,
a milkmaid.—*Yam*, eat, to stuff lustily.—*Yarmouth capon*, a red herring.
—*Znees*, frost, or frozen.—*Zneesy weather*, frosty weather.

THE END.

Printed by Hodgson & Co. 10, Newgate-street, London.

Milton Keynes UK
Ingram Content Group UK Ltd.
UKHW050952110624
443837UK00007B/248

9 781535 806350